Y0-BFY-157

10-B-Y-13.

On Solitude

poems by

Nadine Rae Chapman

Finishing Line Press

Georgetown, Kentucky

On Solitude

for my father and mother

and for John

This is a limited collector's edition.

Copyright © 2005 by Nadine Rae Chapman
ISBN 1-932755-87-X First Edition

All rights reserved under International and Pan-American Copyright Conventions. No part of this book may be reproduced in any manner whatsoever without written permission from the publisher, except in the case of brief quotations embodied in critical articles and reviews.

ACKNOWLEDGMENTS

Grateful acknowledgment is made to the following publications in whose pages these poems first appeared, sometimes in slightly different form:

The Lyric: "A Little House"
Idaho's Poetry: "On Solitude"
Yankee Magazine: "Shadows"

Editor: **Leah Maines**

Author and Cover Photos: **Rick Singer**
                          @RICKSINGERPHOTOGRAPY.COM

Printed in the USA on acid free paper. ♻

Order online: **www.finishinglinepress.com**
                also available on amazon.com

Author inquiries and mail orders:

**Finishing Line Press
P. O. Box 1626
Georgetown, Kentucky 40324
U. S. A.**

Table of Contents

POEM FOR MY MOTHER

Mother stay
tell your body
to wait while the blood builds
wait until fresh forces
arrive to battle your paleness
your unsteady gait
and trembling hands

The bones refuse to hide—
skin falls away
like collapsing memories

But the poppies are blooming
orange
So what if the fragile petal
falls by morning
one leaf of a tome
offered just for a day

Wait
let me read the next page

    *   *   *

Red roses—
how you longed for their scent
the velvet warmth

But we lived with snow
a short
        cool summer
like one slice of lemon
in iced tea

You settled for the pink
wild rose

                    single petals
rose hip jelly
and a husband off
with a bush pilot or at sea

Then you cuddled us
let us share your wide bed
one at a time

One night you stroked
the rose flesh inside your arm
took its fragrance
This is my favorite part
you said

Then I knew I would always
love the body

        *   *   *

You are a Russian box
        black—with one myth or another
        painted on the lid
Today it's a firebird
tomorrow three wishes granted by goldfish
        Magical cities emerge in the distance
        A carved ship sails
        on a scalloped sea
We jiggle and jiggle to pry open the lid
        the insides
        lacquered brilliant red

        *   *   *

I am six Mother
and out of chaos come
the cries of my brother

He has pushed
chunks of wild game
into the grinder

with his finger
Now blood tendon skin
of his four-year-old hand
mingle with moose
and suet

You wrap him in blankets
for comfort
his agony
a slow poison moving
through all of our limbs

You take him into the night
I kneel at the couch
with a sitter
and pray

I should have known you say
Guilt creeps through the halls
fogs up the windows
My brother's hand stays four forever

He learns to shoot—
ptarmigan moose caribou bear—
my father's cure for a sickly son
But the war gods of Vietnam
want the trigger finger perfect
He stays

Today my brother holds your hand
with his shriveled one
promises to take you home
after your last transfusion
How little we understand

Life
for the price of a finger

HE PLAYED AN OBOE . . .

He played an oboe
not a flute
so her parents missed the cues
thinking a child might find
the instrument magic
but not follow the craggy-faced
master of low tones

A Baroque minuet—
was it La Folia—
slipped from the studio window
the day she entered
her shyness wrapped
in gray wool
chilled by snow

With sheet music balanced
against his wrought iron stand
she tried to blow
through double reeds

Breathing exercises
he said

He could help her form
beautiful sounds
only if she would fold
her slight body
rag doll like
over the chair back

He would make talent bloom
in a thousand white blossoms
only if she would bend—
curls limp on the seat
skinny legs dangling

The first touch so light
she hardly knew—

Tone is all in the breath
he said

By the time finches flew
from the lilac hedge
outside the studio window—
their feathers beating brown
puddle water like oars in a race—
she could breath
to the master's beat

His hand more incisive now

His hand unyielding

The force of the breath

The breath

And the hand

Ramming and jamming

the tone and beauty

right out of her

SHADOWS . . .

Shadows fall here
It is past the moment
of pure sunlight

A pine sends its double
across the snow
content to let us think

we feel the piercing
hardness of a cone
or smell sap

A shadow calls us back
into the forest   intimates
a rhythm of the whole

It is a silhouette
not the tree
we know

THIRTEEN . . .

Thirteen—a frenzied gyrator
with hands to the hoop
or drum sticks beating St. Anger

Thirteen—and poised for death
by a tiny pink pouch
vermiform appendix
enraged and unrepentant

If you had been born in the Ice Age
or served as a knight's liege
this would be it

There's no assuaging the mini-despot
nothing to stop the pain
Your smooth child skin
is slit and stapled

While your mother lives
in the circle of wait
her vision of terrors
more vivid than grunge rock
or sci fi imaginings

I DID NOT SLEEP . . .

I did not sleep like the hermits
    beside an open   hand hewn coffin
    or pile skulls   like the monks of Mt. Atmos
    in an earthen room close enough
    to hear wisdom whisper
    to remember my mortality

I blocked out death   distracted by need
    night feedings laundry—colors whites

I took a break from terrors   moved away
    from sinking boats matchstick planes   hunters lost
    in my own frozen wilderness of childhood

No past fears waylaid new labors and dreams
    night vigils—a child's fever
                   croup
                   wet sheets
                   moist thighs
                   scribbled journals
                   fresh jealousies

Our fighting and shriving   the money grind
    a child's deceit   did not rupture the vision
    life as a refinishing—a scouring down
    rubbing new oil into old wounds—
    to recover the sheen

I blocked out death until two figures
    gazed at me from the magic mirror—
    her back half corkscrews his hair
    and grip recede They tender the gift
    Their image and timbre
    are mine in thirty years or less

FIRST THE PHILOSOPHER . . .

I

First the philosopher comes
sporting a tweed coat and beret
beside paradoxes

then the mathematician
with formulas
for function and infinity

and last the farmer
dragging boots through rutted earth
but certain of the resurrection

II

Joy leaves the saint speechless
while the devil sits in the choir loft

III

The ballerina's one-legged soldier
made of tin is called
an accident of casting

not fit for duty in the regiment
but in his love
he stands

THE BELLS OF ST. AUGUSTINE . . .

Cantor

The bells of St. Augustine ring
a call to prayer before the hour

Assembly

The bells of St. Augustine ring

Cantor

In San Joaquin swollen grapes
spill their testimony
in unpolished purple notes

Assembly

The bells of St. Augustine ring

Cantor

My sister's child dances
in a chartreuse light
the filtered light of grapevines

Assembly

The bells of St. Augustine ring

Cantor

My sister's child fries
tortillas   beans
The grape sun fries
her tawny skin to black

Assembly

The bells of St. Augustine ring

Cantor

She rides through fields
in a pick-up bed
a journey bound by fulsome rhythms

Assembly

The bells of St. Augustine ring

Cantor

After harvest
the golden foliage drops
in silent bright staccatos

Assembly

The bells of St. Augustine ring

Cantor

In chary vigil
from their lonely tower
the bells of St. Augustine ring

MARCH . . .

March travels
a barren buckled road
and plays the trickster

March sets up an ice wall
then brings out the thaw
pleads with each bud
to expose desire   receive
his warm embrace

March turns his back
a sudden chill
Hail strikes new growth
while cherry blossoms crumple
on the concrete walk

HAYING TIME . . .

Haying time—tractors move
through acres in hours   fields
cut   hay baled and stacked in days

Horse-drawn sickles and wagons
no longer fill a barnyard
Computer chips   hydraulics

command implements   men
But women still drive truck
after a day's work   Alfalfa

still blooms beside brome   brings
a deep redolence   Rain halts
the cutting   dark purple buds

burst to flower   Storms
tousle crimped windrows
like a farm boy's bleached hair

leave the hay's underside
blackened with mold   Even now
mice tunnel labyrinths

nest under bales   An owl
sits on a fence post   turns its head
from front to back in moonlight

BETWEEN US . . .

Between us lies the Necromancer
Prophetess of Doom   the mistress
who defines your mood
and scoffs at all resistance

Queen of the Night without a high note
she wraps you in her sly embrace
then clamps the heart flow
to dampen all desire

It will not do

I've sent you to the workshop
told the elves to split your sternum
clamp off the vessels of your hardened heart
and fashion new ones

They'll open the spigots
then wire you shut
take back your paleness
the crushing chest pain

Death with her perfect nape and sculpted legs
will have to wait

THE PARTY'S LAST CARNATION . . .

The party's last carnation garnishes an ice pick
dropped   no doubt   by the man
who dances without music

The moon disapproves
and may not appear for a week

She doesn't deserve such a spectacle
a man who feels rhythms are all in his head
a flower impaled on steel
not one true note
to entice

silence out of its dread

SUN I'M TAKING YOU IN LIKE A LEMON . . .

Sun I'm taking you in like a lemon
feasting on your tart ecstasy
your brazen disregard for lesser flavors
like Jupiter or Plato and other far-flung
orbiters who fail to make the grade

Sun cozy up to me today   teach me
how to dabble in the limelight
without succumbing to the Mars play—
always on the cold side—
or sucking up and ending fried

Sun retain your piquant aftertaste
Spike the punch and dash the gray

YOU LIKE TO FLY AT NIGHT . . .

You like to fly at night
the calmest time and cool
no threat of thermals   downdrafts

For you the elements connect
at angles far above the earth
Despite motion sickness
fear of heights
I must scope the North Sky
night dance with you
across a floorless stage

A midnight sun blazes
over the Alaska Range
At cruising altitude
we burst onto the Yukon Basin
Double vision
In your face joy fractures fear
and carries me away

POEM I HAVEN'T GOT TIME FOR YOU . . .

Poem I haven't got time for you
a colicky baby who won't go to bed
you're making my head spin
and the world's in a stew—age after age
stuck in a roomful of toddlers who fight
over red blocks when green ones would do
Scott jams a stick in Alice's eardrum
Fran gouges out Peter's eye with a spoon

Poem shake loose
I'm worn out with being the referee
I'm looking for something sublime
like sassafras tea or mint juleps
something to sip by rose bowers
or at least in the shade of a sycamore tree

Poem stop pounding my head with your rhythms
bizarre metaphors   strange juxtapositions
No more marathon sessions—it's late
I have to be up by six   take out
the garbage   start breakfast
For once stop projecting new worlds
and settle for less

THIS IS YOUR NIGHTMARE . . .

This is your nightmare—
a woman walking out the door

This is your picture
framed and hung—
three eagles stone cut in green
with all the motion
in the patterning
The lines for feathers and beak
rip and bind but drive these birds
Trapped in the print
they never find release

Passion keeps us
in a vortex
of beating wings

IT IS IN THE WAY OF LUMINOUS THINGS . . .

It is in the way of luminous things
that out of darkness   they beckon

Silence is golden   my father said
We lowered the volume
when anger dragged on his lip
But gold   after all   is a cold hard thing
It no longer becomes a woman
and one smile no longer outlasts
all the odd shifting sorrows

The moon's had a face
since I don't know when
It's illuminated   like a woman's

I HAVE A LITTLE HOUSE . . .

I have a little house
sitting on a lawn
The leaves fall on the street
Summer heat is gone

Juniper grows by the rail—
a porch covers the door
Bookshelves slump back to back
The chairs are stuffed and bored

The piano hugs an inside wall—
a light weeps on the keys
A mantle caps the brick fireplace
each photograph looks pleased

Linoleum creeps along the hall
The cupboards guard their store
Two small windows screen the world—
through slats the sun is floored

Stairs rise up in Yankee blue
The fenced-in yard is bare
Leaves wither on the walk—
I must love from here

KODIAK. . .

Kodiak
like so many others
we dropped anchor
out of need for safe harbor

The fishermen   repairing nets
on those gray gray days
gazed at our fourteen foot sloop

They saw four children
a mother wild-eyed
from sudden rough waters
through Shelikof Strait

I don't recall
the ocean treating us
like riffraff

I had too much faith
in my father
or was it terror's way
to spare me the memory

I do see
my mother below deck   praying
Two small children kneel—
their heads in her lap
their bodies under the skeletal
grip of her hands

That image remains
a fishhook I've swallowed
that no longer twists gut
but tears at the heart wall

ON SOLITUDE

Woman washing tiles
each day you come
to the convent's walkway
splash your holy water
upon a baked brick
landscape   Some laugh
at cracks that gleam
out penance in the face
of wise men's dirty feet
or frown at wasted work
Sisters even call you "fool"
-try to reason life
off reddened knees
Your eyes rise up
from cushions of advanced age
calling back accusers
Though you never speak
many listen on the hidden
stairwells of your labor

About the Author

Nadine Chapman teaches creative writing and composition at Whitworth College in Spokane, Washington. She is also a registered nurse. Her creative nonfiction will appear in *At Work in Life's Garden: Writers on the Spiritual Adventure of Parenting* (EWU Press, 2005).

Chapman earned an MFA degree from Eastern Washington University in 1996. She spent her childhood in Anchorage, Alaska and on the Aleutian Islands, where her father operated a cattle ranch. Before teaching writing, she worked as a psychiatric nurse. She lives with her husband and children in Spokane and often travels to their farm on the Camas Prairie in Idaho. Her stories about women living there have appeared in *Weber Studies and Frontiers: A Journal of Women Studies.*